To See the Earth

PHILIP METRES

D1157416

Cleveland State University Poetry Center
Cleveland, Ohio
IMAGINATION SERIES #12

LCCN 2007050995
ISBN 978-1-880834-71-8

This book is a title in the **imagination** series published
by the Cleveland State University Poetry Center,
2121 Euclid Avenue, Cleveland OH 44115-2214.

Book design by BookMatters, Berkeley
Set in Adobe Garamond
Cover design by Frank Cucciarre, Blink Concept

Library of Congress Cataloging-in-Publication Data

Metres, Philip, 1970-
    To see the earth / Philip Metres.
        p. cm. — (Imagination series ; # 12)
    ISBN 978-1-880834-71-8 (alk. paper)
    I. Title. II. Series.
PS3613.E887T6 2008
811'.6—dc22   2007050995

To See the Earth

Other Books by Philip Metres

POETRY
Instants (chapbook)
Primer for Non-Native Speakers (chapbook)

TRANSLATION
A Kindred Orphanhood: Poems of Sergey Gandlevsky
Catalogue of Comedic Novelties: Selected Poems
of Lev Rubinstein

CRITICISM
Behind the Lines: War Resistance Poetry on
the American Homefront since 1941

ACKNOWLEDGMENTS

Grateful acknowledgment is due to the following journals and anthologies for publishing versions of these poems:

America	"Nicodemus Below the Cross: Votive Ivory on Display"
Artful Dodge	"Letter to My Sister"
Bat City Review	"Two States (Graduation Day, 2005)"
Big Bridge	"one more story he said In a Restaurant in Amsterdam"
Crab Orchard Review	"Negatives"
DIAGRAM	"Ascent" (part of "A House Without")
	"Inheritance" (part of "A House Without")
	"Post-Soviet Sestina"
Field	"Antibodies (for Adele)"
	"The Familiar Pictures of Dis"
	"Echolocation Islands"
Literal Latte	"Primer for Non-Native Speakers"
Mizna	"The Ash Tree"
	"Patronymic"
New England Review	"Ashberries: Letters"
	"Making Meshi"
	"Hiroshima: A Panorama"

North Dakota Review	"On 24th and South, Philadelphia"
Poetry	"The Ballad of Skandar"
Prairie Schooner	"St. Basil"
	"Days of 1993"
River Styx	"From Sokolniki"
	"For the Fifty (Who Made PEACE with Their Bodies)"
Seneca Review	"Memory Jar" (part of "A House Without")
Tin House	"Bat Suite"
	"Stopping by Krispy Kreme"

"Ashberries: Letters" was reprinted in *Best American Poetry 2002*; "Ashberries: Letters," "The Ballad of Skandar," and "Making Meshi," also will appear in *Arab American and Diaspora Literature Anthology*; parts of "A House Without" and "Post-Soviet Sestina" also appeared in *DIAGRAM: Selections from the Magazine and More*; "Ashberries: Letters," "A House Without," and "one more story he said In a restaurant in Amsterdam" also appeared in *Inclined to Speak: Contemporary Arab American Poetry*.

Grateful acknowledgment is also due to the Wick Poetry Series for publishing the chapbook *Primer for Non-Native Speakers* (Kent State University Press, 2004), where some of these poems first appeared.

Thanks to Maggie Anderson, Cathy Bowman, Mark Halliday, Roger Mitchell, Maura Stanton, and especially my advisors David Wojahn and Bob Cording for your guidance and sage advice. Thanks as well to Abner Bardeguez, Jenny Barker, Becca Black, Jim Doppke, Chris Green, Bob King, Mike Magee, E.J. McAdams, Paula McLain, Anna Meek, Drew Morse, Tyrone Simpson, Gigi Thibodeaux, and my family (Dad, Mom, Kath, Dave)—all of whom read versions of the manuscript.

Thanks to Dmitry Psurtsev, Sergey Gandlevsky, Olga Leontevna, the Maslov family, John Patton, Paul and Mary Asel, Bernie Sucher, Jeff Lilley, Jeremy Huck, Peter Rossi, the Thomas J. Watson Foundation, and all the other fellow travelers (Willem, Mike, Nina, Steve, Tom, Garrick—you know who you are) who made my life in Russia possible. Thanks as well to Majed Abbadi, Kathryn Bryan, Khuloud Jaqaman, Rima Kapitan, Kadhim Shabaan, Vera Tamari, and the Cleveland Friends Meeting.

Thanks to Indiana University, John Carroll University, Ledig House, and the Ohio Arts Council, for supporting the writing of this manuscript.

Special thanks to Michael Dumanis and Rita Grabowski at the Cleveland State Univeristy Poetry Center, to BookMatters for book design, and Frank Cucciarre of Blink Concept for the cover design.

Thank you, finally, to my wife Amy Breau, and our daughters Adele and Leila, without whom this would not have been.

for my family

Since in my sight, you see the earth again,

Cleared of its stiff and stubborn, man-locked set,
And, in my hearing, you hear its tragic drone

Rise liquidly in liquid lingerings
Like watery words awash; like meanings said

By repetitions of half-meanings.

WALLACE STEVENS
"Angel Surrounded by Paysans"

CONTENTS

Primer for Non-Native Speakers   *3*

I

Ashberries: Letters   *11*
Ashberries: A Spectroscopy   *14*
Days of 1993   *15*
Yuri Gagarin's Spaceship   *18*
Matryoshka, Memory   *20*
Echolocation Islands   *24*
From Sokolniki   *27*
Reunion: Insomnia Dacha   *28*
Post-Soviet Sestina   *30*

II

Patronymic   *35*
Stopping By Krispy Kreme   *37*
Letter to My Sister   *40*
Making Meshi   *43*
The Ballad of Skandar   *45*
A House Without   *47*
The Familiar Pictures of Dis   *51*
Two States (Graduation Day, 2005)   *54*
Installation/Occupation   *55*
The Ash Tree   *57*

III

St. Basil *63*
On 24th and South, Philadelphia *67*
Hiroshima: A Panorama *69*
The Idle Childless *71*
Negatives *72*
Creation Story on Magnolia Drive, Cleveland *74*
Nicodemus Below the Cross: A Votive Ivory *76*
Antibodies (for Adele) *78*
one more story he said In a restaurant in Amsterdam *83*
For the Fifty (Who Made PEACE with Their Bodies) *84*
Bat Suite *87*

Notes *91*

To See the Earth

Primer for Non-Native Speakers

I.

This is an apple. What is it?
A table. Some bread and tea.

II.

And this? This is a ruble,
a rue, a wish I could sell you
exactly what I feel.
A double negative: if you can't
not speak, then write. Sit and eat
the peeled apple in your hand.

III.

I understand X,
but cannot speak Y.

Possessive phrases: he has,
she has, I don't have.
Look, I lack,
says my language.

IV.

My language—

 A heavy winter coat,
          tight in the shoulders.
Sour apples,

plucked by the breeze.
Dirt stars,
          smudges on knees.

v.

My camera is broken.
Can you sing? Where can I
hang my coat?

vi.

The titmouse chitter
          before song.

The mad clap
          and wingstutter

of lifting pigeons,
          an asthmatic's wheeze.

vii.

A line at the beer kiosk—
discourse in the past perfect,
the present imperfect.
Questions in the future indefinite.

viii.

He missed his love.
He brought with him.
The sun already set.

He wound up at the station.
An inopportune time.

"They beat you
because of your face,
not because of your passport."

IX.

I have a few questions
of a personal nature:
Where is the toilet?
How many acts in this play?
What is the rate of exchange?
Where does this street lead?
When is my turn?
You come after the speaker from Bulgaria.
Who is speaking now?
Could you speak
even slower?

X.

Prepositions governing
the accusative, the simple superlative
of adjectives. The Moscow Metro
is a most punctual subway.
It is also most busy. I've lost
my reflexive pronoun
many times among the

babushkas, bags, dacha bicycles,
drunks and dogs.

XI.

Would you like to see
Yuri Gagarin's spaceship?

Would you like to visit
the Exhibition of the National
Economic Achievements
of the U.S.S.R.?

At the Metro entrance,
babushkas scolding
other people's children,
someone selling fresh eggs,
pickled cukes, kittens in a coat,
and where the blast of cold
meets the Metro heat,
the wordless pleading
of a blind pensioner.

XII.

Reticence of winter streets.

XIII.

The constant stress of simple comparative:
ours, yours, ours, yours.

XIV.

And in a dark stairwell, smell
of drying urine,
the light bulb stolen
again this week.

XV.

And in a dark stairwell,
a stone-drunk body.
Iambic steps now running up stairs,
the swear
of a slammed door.

XVI.

And in a dark stairwell,
a cry—
she's just learned the language
of *rigor mortis*,
then teaches the drunk

the declensions
of an outraged woman's fists.

XVII.

If anyone asks for me,
I'm in Chapter Ten.

XVIII.

This is a label. What is it?
A libel, a labia, a lust, alleluia.

XIX.

And this?   A table.
Some bread and a plea.

XX.

Please.
What is it?
You are wanted on the phone.
There is no dial tone.
The telephone is out of order.
I'll be waiting for your call.

XXI.

Goodbye, dear friends.
I wish you every success.
Have a safe journey.
Please stay.

XXII.

Let me introduce myself.
I feel sick.
How much must I pay
for excess baggage?

I

It's time to change the record—but I'm dreaming again
Of the motherland. Bored, shouldering past crowds
At the station, I wait for the train, since I intend to grow
Some apples or gooseberries. September's leaving.
I dream that I'm dreaming of crossing a wide country . . .
SERGEY GANDLEVSKY

Ashberries: Letters

Outside, in a country with no word
for *outside*, they cluster on trees,

red bunches. I looked up
ryabina, found *mountain ash*. No

mountains here, just these berries
cradled in yellow leaves.

When I rise, you fall asleep. *We
barely know each other*, you said

on the phone last night. Today, sun brushes
the wall like an empty canvas, voices

from outside drift into this room. I can't
translate—my words, frostbitten

fingers. I tell no one how your hands
ghost over my back, letters I hold.

2.

Reading children's stories by Tolstoy,
Alyosha traces his index

over the alphabet his mouth so easily
unlocks. Every happy word resembles

every other, every unhappy word's
unhappy in its own way. Like apartments

at dusk. Having taken a different street
from the station, I was lost in minutes.

How to say, where's the street like this,
not this? Keys I'd cut for years coaxed open

no pursed lips. How to say, blind terror?
Sprint, lungburn, useless tongue? How say

thank you, muscular Soviet worker, fading
on billboard, for pointing me the way?

3.

Alyosha and I climbed trees to pick berries, leaves
almost as red. On ladders, we scattered

half on the ground, playing who could get them
down the other's shirt without their knowing.

Morning, the family gone, I ground the berries
to skin, sugared sour juices twice.

Even in tea they burned. In the yard,
leafpiles of fire. Cigarettes between teeth,

the old *dvorniks* rake, scratch the earth,
try to rid it of some persistent itch.

I turn the dial, it drags my finger back.
When the phone at last connects to you, I hear

only my own voice, crackle of the line.
The rakes scratch, flames hiss and tower.

4.

This morning, the trees bare. Ashberries
on long black branches. Winter. My teacher

says they sweeten with frost, each snow
a sugar. Each day's dark grows darker,

and streets go still, widen, like ice over lakes,
and words come slow to every chapped mouth,

not just my own, having downed a little vodka
and then some tea. Tomorrow I'll bend down

branches, brittle with cold, pluck what I can't
yet name, then jar the pulp and save the stones.

What to say? Love, I live for the letters
I must wait to open. They bear across

this land, where I find myself at a loss—
each word a wintering seed.

Ashberries: A Spectroscopy

There is a word for outside. When you say outside, you say on the street, even where there is no street outside, just a dirt path. To take off your shoes and don slippers, when entering from the street that is no street.

Down the street that was a street, past the train station, in a town that had been closed to foreigners during the Cold War (the site of the Russian space program), the School of Forest Technology allowed me, an alien, to scrimmage with their varsity basketball squad. After practice, the boys pulled out Marlboros and smoked, naked in locker room haze. Once a cow wandered through the center of campus. Getting lost requires a sense of place in the first place.

Fall 1992. The Russian economy was a tree, losing all its leaves at once. Alyosha played "Born to Run" when picking ashberries. The first snow: October 12th. I went to Russia because poetry was said to matter there. When I said this, my hosts chuckled. *Poetry is okay, but it can't buy sausage.*

Dima read the poem. *This is your myth of Russia, not Russia.* When I told my hosts I was moving out, their faces turned into icons. On the street, the wooden faces lay on tables. One poet's life savings of rubles, stuffed in a mattress, now could not buy a sausage. The first word I did not know was *arbuz.* A big apple, they explained. Driving off the airport highway, we pulled up to a line of trucks, their mouths spilling open with the *big apples.* On the ride home, we spat watermelon seeds out the window, onto the street.

Days of 1993

1.

Akhmatova touches her neck, as if to protect
were no different than to choke, looks over her bare shoulder
to the unseen photographer, eyes aglimmer, as if

I were a burning city. As if she imagined the other
me, squinting through cracked taxi windshield, pointing out
the Kremlin to visiting parents. *Is this the country we feared?*

my dad asked, an ex-Cold Warrior aghast at the rutted
airport runway, at a Muscovite's habit of turning off
headlights at night on an open road, at the dual use

of newsprint in the toilet—to peruse and wipe your ass with.
In Vietnam, he'd marveled at teeming streets, difficulty
of completing even a phone call: *To get anything done,*

he'd joked then, *it would take an act of Congress.* Thirty years
    later,
listening to the tapes he'd sent home, it came to him
—once, rushing back by Jeep to base at night, armed

only with his horn, he aimed for a strait between crowds,
    gunned it,
and plowed into a cycling woman. *I'm sorry*, he said, *I'm sorry*,
over and over, wheels still spinning on an upended bike.

2.

The Muscovites and I trudge along gray ice, mime one another's
every solid step, when a tinted Mercedes roars past—

anonymity and speed. Someone curses, someone shakes
her head, another gazes as if at an unrequited love,

as if at another world. For a time, I tried to hide
among them, trading my American years—inevitability

of winter fruit, hot showers, electricity—for days
spent searching for oranges, days spent formulating

a request for bread, black bread, please. Days spent negotiating
the inscrutable queue, logic of purchase, dizzying

inflating ruble. Once, drunk with fatigue, I stumbled
onto the tall windows of a Western grocery, found myself

unable to enter. Ceiling lights too bright, shelves full
of multicolored pasta boxes, pornography of chocolate.

3.

Before I left America the first time, the wise advised:
pantyhose, Levi's, Chanel No. 5. Russians are starved
for that stuff. Where there is demand, a market comes. My
    second trip,

years later, I read in the English-language *Moscow Times*:
Glasnost gals! Visit our website, and click on the face. Couldn't
sleep. On TV: Playboy's "Girls of the Car Wash" deliver

trademarked fantasies, their breathless voices overdubbed
by Russian baritone, astral snow, and a Hollywood film, full of
blondes, Uzis and jewels. Unseen, daughters of the Vietcong

make a buck a day stitching and gluing the same Nike sneakers
that will get a kid killed in Cabrini Green, where I walk,
oblivious to Chicago's neighborhood borders.

How would Akhmatova describe this? Who would listen today
to a prophet like Amos? *We buy the poor for shoes, the needy
for a pair of sandals.* What hands have touched these boots I
    can't tell,

but in subways they took in so many gazes, I felt half-crazy, half-
possessed in possessing, traces ghosting everything
I own. On the radio below Akhmatova's eyes,

a voice: *Seven billion dollars annual in trafficking
of human beings.* Perhaps right now, a woman gathers
some clothes together with her courage, takes the job

beyond her imagining: Hong Kong, New York, Amsterdam.
When I gave up trying to live "like a Russian," I'd sit
at the Pushkin Square McDonald's among Russians,

translating poems, trying to crack their Cyrillic codes. Billions
and billions sold. I'd buy a burger—its mediocrity at least

familiar. Across the road, I'd almost see bronze Pushkin
staring down. Traffic streaming between poet and golden arches.

Yuri Gagarin's Spaceship

No detailed pictures of Soviet space
ships were ever released: thus, this artist's

conception on the Jell-O box is pure
conjecture: it looks like a telescope,

half-collapsed, eye-windowed, just a soup can
nesting inside a soup can, Warhol

meets Matryoshka Doll. It's alright, Mama,
I'm only flying in my *umwelt*, outside

of which there is no breathing. The world
is its own best representation: .

Sputnik, Vostok, Soyuz, the troubled
space station *Mir*—in metallic skin, I can't make out

the miners digging coal for spaceship steel
I only imagine to see the earth

from. What's this blue—violet—absolute
block? Traveler, wherever you flee, there

you are. Columbus of the Cosmos, you discovered
drops of water float inside "like butterflies,"

while your Vostok hurtled eighteen thousand miles
per hour. No pup tent you slept one year in,

snuggling the airstrip's Whitmanic line,
like Lowell on Allen Tate's Tennessee lawn—

beyond the gravity well, you orbited
the globe like an eyeball shucked from its socket,

shedding your father's cabinets and bricks,
your mother's milk. *Traveler, Eastward, Union.*

It's a small capsule you are swallowed in.
The globe's a ball we spin while standing

still. On the axis of a single finger,
the pen still needs the dumb thumb to guide it

through white space, so starved of oxygen
it begins to spot black. Yuri, I've yet to see

your spaceship, your mythic, your extra
-ordinary frame outside the frame of things

from which everything suddenly appears
as it is, beyond death, how you see us

now, after your plane gave birth to shrapnel
and flame . . . I cradle a key-chain globe, eye-

sized. Like Baba Yaga's hut, it sprouts hidden
chicken legs when it hears the secret rhyme,

it holds at least thirty rooms, throat gardens,
neck of the words, fountains of wine.

Matryoshka, Memory

We were four sisters, four sisters were we. . . .
Perhaps we were not four, but five.
MIKHAIL KUZMIN

I.

I had to enter four locked doors
to see my grandfather. We colored ducks

any color, just trying to keep within the lines.
He loved blue ducks, so ducks were blue

until blue ran out. We worked shapes,
their names hazy, into the places meant

for them. He kept forcing *circle*
into *square*. Around us, in squares,

another patient wouldn't stop walking,
her every step retracing lines she made

each day and each day her mind erased.

2.

Inside, where bay opened past bay
windows, Grandpa sat, rocking himself

like a mother and child. My mother recalled
our day to him—awakening to salt breezes,

the bleached white shoreline churches
against the almost painful glitter of breakers.

Unmoored from words, his face still spoke—
the waves stinging his eyes to tears.

Soon, in the wake of his brain, he will lose
the harbor, a daughter's face. His sea legs leave.

His hands will anchor to his lap. Soon, the world
will narrow to a bed, bread taken through a tube.

Mercy, mercy when he forgets, at last, to breathe.

3.

Cut
from linden
branch, stripped of
bark, it's set to lathe,
turned and turned—
until, like a child, it can't
remember how to stand. Hand-
painted, then lacquered, each one nests
inside taller, shapelier others. Which doll's
mother to them all? Its simple expression
refuses to answer. It might bear, instead,
across its generous belly, a flowering lily
or a starch-white church, identical cupolas
glinting in a barren field. How is it I
ever fit so easily into myself?

4.

Each day I pass the lilies nailed
to this wall still splintered

by the car's impact. A new bouquet
each day. Someone's written

*I love you Sasha and will always
remember.* Every day I remember

words for the simplest things: *rain,
waiting, grandfather, umbrella, twilight,*

horizon. But last night, when the bus
arrived, a man with one leg hoisted himself

halfway in, then, knocked back
by umbrellas and elbows, fell

into me. The bus left. He crutched himself
back up, dusted his coat. We waited.

Echolocation Islands

With echoes, a blind traveler can perceive
complex, detailed, and specific information
from distances far beyond the reach
of the longest cane or arm . . .

1. *Elk Island*

The lost eye lands   its lusty lens
wherever it finds   an impression:

here, below the canopy of sky
-shouldering trees, the old folk

search on their knees
for mushrooms, hushed rooms

between the fields and cities.
This is *Losiny Ostrov*, Elk Island,

pillared aisles of birch and pine,
lost islands of light arcing

into sight. Half-blinded, I can't see
how tanks could have pulled down

this heaven, islets the eye lets in
and the islets that inlet the eye.

2. *Elk Island (2)*

Eye, find a place to get lost. *Ostrov*,
you are all you have been, site

of troop maneuvers and mushroom
hunting, a maze of hidden dens

and open fields unscrolling, rolling . . .
now surrounded by a frozen plain

you lie, lost island of elk, birch
like bleached ribs bared to air. I hear

your branches clack like antennae,
see them snag the yolk of moon, sky

spilling into facets of light. I see a sea
that is no sea, churned and frozen

white. Island, I don't see where you end,
unbroken amnesia of snow.

3. *Solovki*

Every island is a main, undone
by. Every one is a word

some eye can unsay. Such as: *you
are an enemy of.* Or: *you are no one.*

Pages torn out, washed away.
Millions of ears and what is heard?

Some unwording cry I
cannot fix into form. Such as:

(
and: (

The dead voices loiter, edge
the island unsighted. History is

the sea slapping the mute shore,
sapping the shore of the shore.

From Sokolniki

On Moscow's outskirts, falcon and falconer
once stretched the orbit of trust. They've left
only the name, *sokol'nik*, lost circles from sky
to departed hand. Last orange light

washes through trees tugged by wind. A friend
chops carrots, I slice apples, cramped around the table.
He tells of a strange book—a single word
repeated for two hundred pages. (He'd forgotten

the word). Reporters crowded, the writer spoke:
*Every morning, alone, before light, I'd begin
yearning for the word. As I wrote, I'd lose it,
then find it along the way. At times I'd feel*

*miles from it, then next to it, then I would hate it
the way you can hate someone you've loved
enough to let go. But it stayed. And here we are.*
The sun is lost now, under the blue of new snow.

Somewhere, lovers touch tenderly in the dark
as if their bodies were bruised, as if they spoke
different languages. As if they did not know
what days would bring, and they could lose

each other, the thread of a word fluttering
so awkwardly between them. A word
they did not know they already knew, and would
repeat, until even their names were gone.

Reunion: Insomnia Dacha

How to say *spider* again?
    Storms & *drunkards* crawl
my tongue instead.

How to say *where I am*
    from? We drank hours ago.
Words still buzz the palate:

the Estonian poet
    uncorking a Russian bottle
into Japanese glasses—

"around the table
    we share
pure spirits"—

vodka (brother to *vodá*,
    water) warming the chest
like a *banya*, bathhouse—

after-dinner *chai*,
    leaves spinning in the cup
the steam swirls above—

while outside, the *paúk*
    unplucks its web thread by thread
as the storm comes on—

wherever *paúk* fingers
        its way, "spider" creeps the center
of gossamer *paútina*—

In this country, where "rain"
        lies in "wait" & "memories"
petrify into "monuments,"

where *soznaniye* borders
        "consciousness" & "conscience,"
a spider fires its strands

by heart, *bezsonnitsa*
        sprawling between
"sleepless" & "dreamless" . . .

Post-Soviet Sestina

October 1996

The light wakes me, the alarm did not. Bad sign,
it's six and I've got an eight o'clock flight.
Outside, Sasha's stuttering that my phone line
was dead, the traffic's bad, his Volga cab
sputters from the cold. My suitcases form
a perfect wall around me, Cold War border

in the vinyl backseat. Sasha borders
on the politely apoplectic. Signs
read *Moscow City Limits*. Billboards form
a history of the moment—the flight
from crowded train to Mercedes cab,
communal apartment to credit line.

Disaster: my fate is not in the line
on my palm, or in the stars. It borders
the road—a single nail. Now Sasha's cab
and my plans read just like the blind man's signs
at the mouth of the Metro: . The flight
from Moscow leaves without me. It's poor form

to overstay your welcome, when the forms
say by such and such date on the dotted line
you must leave this world. But that first flight's
the last today over the Russian border.
So I take a bus back, pass again the sign
City Limits, not enough cash for a cab.

I borrow a hundred from a friend, take a cab
back to the dark apartment, and inform
my love at home by phone that it's a sign
I must've left something behind. The phone line
hisses between us. I'm on the border
of a mind like two countries. Thoughtflight

at midnight. I wake. And won't miss this flight,
already past the *Limits* in Dima's cab.
I reach *Visa Control*. But the border-
guard says I must buy a new visa form
upstairs. Enough time for the ticket line
to close. Okay, I'm desperate now, so I sign

my life away on *Aeroflot*. Planes form
a queue, we taxi on tarmac. Good sign.
We lift in flight. A border's just a line.

II

We move between two darknesses.

E.M. FORSTER

Patronymic

A man named Attalah from Mourjan traced his roots back
to the Ghassassinat—those who'd come from Mesopotamia to
  Lebanon

Eight years old, new to the neighborhood, I pedaled past
a pack of kids: their stare. *Spic. Hey spic.* First one, then a hail
of crabapples pelting my back.

Because of his bravery in wars against the Shi'ites,
the Amir called him Abou Alrijali, "Father of Men"

On a Carnival Cruise, my father once dressed as a sheikh—
as if to unlock what was coiled in cells, buried under tongues.
All junior high I blow-dried the revolt of curls.

From that day forth, he was Abou Alrijali
With print standardization the name became Abourjaili

In England I was French. In France I was Moroccan.
In Russia I was Chechen. In Greece, they read my olive skin
as theirs, could not believe when I couldn't understand.

At Ellis Island, when Skandar ibn Mitri Abourjaili was asked
it was written: Skandar Metres

But at the port near Ephesus, the scrum of drivers
and pickpockets surrounded us, strictly business. Among ruins
of houses, a boy who could pass for my child

pressed an old coin into my hand, asking for nothing
but its value in American. My cousin, forgive me,
I was struck dumb: foreigner to my own lips.

Like yesterday, a Friday, the sun down, a man
in black coat and bowler hat stopped me in the street:
Son, it's time for *shul*. Why do you walk home?

Stopping by Krispy Kreme

On I-65, south of Louisville,
our eyes locked on the totem KRISPY KREME
half lost in a forest of signs, we turned
off the main stream. We'd heard the donut chain's

disappearing. Tucked in a corner,
behind faux-glass double doors, they lay
fluorescent. We ransacked the last row.
On the road, nostalgia, sugar, sixties

tunes: *hit the road, Jack,* Ray's outrage, Martha
and the Vandellas *nowhere to run,*
nowhere to hide. All afternoon, we picked
our way through Broncos and eighteen-wheelers

with sticky hands. At Hodgenville, Lincoln's
birthplace, we rummaged through
chocolate Lincoln, keychain Lincoln,
Lincoln lunchboxes, his face on every wall

watching us. Named after his grandfather,
Abraham, who was killed by an Indian
his father killed one moment later.
In the museum, a facsimile

of a letter. How once, in Kentucky,
Lincoln witnessed a slave caravan
pass through town. On hands and necks
a web of chains, iron collars biting.

At that moment, he saw a family sundered
as easily, perhaps, as we imagine him
hefting his fabled axe. History
is part cartoon, part bloodied tongue:

Mary Todd's madness, presidential
depression, the prurience of news
we abhor and buy. What were the headlines—
why did Booth scream, "*sic semper tyrannus*"?

We pressed *play*, and Lincoln whirred to life,
1863, Gettysburg: "our fathers
brought forth a new nation, conceived
in liberty . . . all men created equal. . . ."

What do we know of Lincoln's mother
the family left, buried in Kentucky?
That she couldn't read. I once asked my mom
what she'd like remembered of her family.

"That's nice, sweetheart," was all she passed on.
In the car, we listened to '68—
letter-tapes my dad sent home, holed up
in a Saigon hotel during Tet,

angular fear in his cool monotone.
As the tape wound down, he invoked his family's
names—*Mom, Dad, Richard, John, Lila-baby*,
as if they formed a mantra strong enough

to hold the VC off. How easy to eject
the tape, ease out of our rental's A/C
into Lincoln's one-windowed shack,
cradled now in pillared limestone.

We walked inside, then quickly out again.
It seemed wrong to gawk at what had been
just a shell from the elements. Outside, wind creaking
cedars. Here, at Sinking Springs, Lincoln

dunked buckets for water. Then they moved,
and moved again, and he to Springfield,
across the country, to Washington,
and finally to Ford Theater, now

a museum diorama where his head
slumps and Mary's mouth gapes open
and open, actors even in the balcony.

Letter to My Sister

Katherine, when you came back
to our oak and maple suburb,
unreal, occupied, you caressed an olive tree
pendant, talked of ancestral homes

bulldozed for settler roads, olive groves
torn from the ground, your Palestinian love
unable to leave, his passport denied
at the airport. He'd never tell what he did

to be detained, words that could be taken
against your will. Instead, he gave you
this olive tree to hang around your neck,
said *A country is more important*

than one person. I don't know.
I've read emails of the new torture—
an overhead projector behind a prisoner,
turned on, until he feels his head

will catch fire. Last week, over baklava
and tea, rain pounding the door,
"Ashraf" spoke of barbed wire, boycotts
and curfews—how his dozen siblings split

into sides. *Israeli soldiers*
hurt you, and we wanted them to hurt.
We couldn't imagine any other way.
I wrote his story down. We met

again. He said I still didn't understand.
He said, *Write me out, keep only*
the general outline, not how I slipped
through checkpoints or where I hid

when they came for us. What I wrote or said,
each revealing detail, could spell
someone's end. When the story appeared
in the *Voice*, he only ghosted its margins, shadow

to a place not fully his. But there's no story
without particulars. What resistance could live
on the stale bread of statistics, the drought
of broken accords? It almost requires

bloodstained walls of a mosque,
prostrate backs shot through—a visible sign
of an invisible disgrace. Today, I open
the newspaper, try to peer between the grain

of a photo: a staggering crowd, arms entwined
and straining, as if to hold something back.
It could be us, facing a danger constantly
off-screen. No, we were born here.

On the stove, potatoes boil.
NPR segues labor strike
and missile strike with witty violin.
Twilight, I'm looking out the window,

trying to strike a few words
into flame. The dark lowers its wet sack,
then hoods the whole house. Outside,
something is falling. I strain to see it

past the glare of the kitchen light.

Making Meshi

I was five, rolling grape leaves
into thick fingers: *meshi*. *Ne touche pas,*
ne touche pas, my father trying to hug

his mother's back, proudly bowed
before the oven. *God-damned French*
hudda. Everyone laughed

when Grandpa swore in Arabic, as if
the language itself were a punch line.
Plucking grape leaves from

the patio vine. Everyone reaching
for words to describe them, all garlic
lemon on the tongue. Why did he talk

to her like that? Washing,
spreading the leaves open,
veins pointed up. Grandma's tongue

a French Beirut convent, Grandpa's tongue
planted between his teeth, biting off
his Arabic. It was pride,

the way they held
or lashed their tongues. Spooning spiced rice
into the palm. Folding the base

inward to center. Grandpa scolded a cusser:
What kind of language is that? Aroma
of arms. Tucking the wings in

—but unwinding, undone in young fingers.
I can't keep them all together. Blanketing the pot
with torn leaves. Years later, lying

in my father's room, in summer's
oven, I heard them, whispering, in their bed. Beyond
the wall, all embers and breathing—

The Ballad of Skandar

Dayr al-Qamar, Lebanon

Unframed by any photograph, diminished by history,
      rehearsed in no song,
embalmed by oral memory, great-grandfather
      where have you gone?

Under the waning moon, in the valley
      of Dayr al-Qamar,
Skandar ibn Mitri—Arab,
      Christian, soldier for the occupier.

In the far margins of the Ottoman Empire,
      above a little town,
a Muslim diverted the living stream,
      the story passes down,

to irrigate his crops. The Christians below
      sent up soldier after soldier:
they couldn't capture the unnamed
      wily Muslim. Until Skandar,

courageous warrior, brought down
      the Muslim in cuffs.
In the village below, gunshots. Skandar
      fell, a bullet in his calf.

The bound Muslim dragged him

safe behind a cedar.
Skandar gave the man his key,
          changed his fate forever.

What would Skandar choose:
          jail or exile? Exile,
at least, is freedom. But where is freedom?
          Beyond the far walls

of the Ottoman empire, a house without
          iron bars on windows,
where water flows from every spout—
          or so the story goes.

A House Without

for Lily Boulos

1.

She leans against the stairwell railing,
trying to catch her breath
as if it were a moth, hovering

around a bulb, just out of reach. Her heart
failing for months now, her lungs exhausted
as night swimmers, arms flailing

the black glass of water for something solid.
The knifepoint of each inhaling.
In the convent, as a teen, she could steal

the ball from any priest and swish a shot
from thirty feet. Now, in her last ascent,
she turns, stares down the dark stairwell

and grabs the rail as if it were the arm
of someone trying to rob her.

2.

Out on our porch, out facing the shapeless
dark of moonless night, our father told us:
his mother still unconscious, he rose
from his childhood bed, the room cluttered

with what he'd always seen as junk, a still life
of Depression shelves brimming with chipped
tea cups and statues hoarded and stirred
to life with prayer to saints she figured

bodily, and good on their promises:
Saint Jude, patron of desperate cases.
Saint Anthony, patron of the lost. Eyes
closed, he could walk each room of that house

in his mind. At the hospital, he found her
sitting up, in a white gown,
still-black hair combed to small shoulders,
looking calmly out the far window, at dawn.

3.

Arches of eyebrows and aisles, stained glass
gaze and minaret mind. Onyx-eyed. You take
everyone in, and raise them. Hands now hidden,
they grow thick in the knuckles, numb to pans

pulled bare from the oven. How did they feel
so tender on my nape of my neck? Faux pearls
and rosaries, sayings and saints and dark
household God—who could ever believe

they know you? You swallow your mother tongue.
One by one we abandon the rooms, and leave
a button you like: *Just Visiting This Planet.*
You always dished out more than we could chew:

the first refusal's politeness. The third is rude.
If you love me, you will have something to eat.
And now you feed the soil. It takes you in.
What house is left without you?

4. *Memory Jar*

Qui se ressemble, s'assemble.
Invitation is the sincerest form
of fluttering. Lily, it's dark
and I can't see you. *La patience
est un virtue.* Cliché, a cocktail dress
you wore to hide your shy desire:
five months pregnant with my father,
you had no idea why you tired
climbing stairs. *When you work,
you have one demon; without work,
you face a thousand.* The dark house
even dark in day. The house in pieces.
A thousand nights torment the lazy

golden silence. My hands grope the walls
in a dark foyer. A house without
children runs away from you. *Qui s'excuse,
s'accuse.* In case of emergency, contact
someone you've never known. I ask
and ask. *Qui ne dit mot, consent.*
When you run after a woman, she runs away
like a house without windows. When you
leave, she pursues you.

The Familiar Pictures of Dis

I.

                         -truction: crushed cars ditches
of roads broken pavement dis-

      }

mantled stone walls   loose cables & clouds
of dust & dirt   an envelope   returning

      }

to sender: no one by that name   still   ill
living & so the dead letter returns

      }

every night the neighbors hiding in houses heard
sounds of smashing   they could not see

      }

what the soldiers hurled through
the windows of the Ministry of Culture

      }

after all something needs to be broken   to cor-   ore
respond   an objective cor

      }

-relative   & sorrow is a house no one
would visit   unless it visits upon one

2.

past midnight   the sound of barking:
a soldier had attached a speaker to a tape

         }

playing a recording of barking dogs   the village
dogs joined   a neighborhood chorus of de-

         }

fense   we will not sleep together   gather
stones   to live in the basin of some ancient

         }

ocean: the stones rise & break   ache
the surface of the earth   this is the holy

         }

riddled with the stones: in the Ministry   tree
they took everything or took stones

         }

to everything: computers cameras photocopiers
chimeras scanners hard   disks smashed or scat

         }

tered   there is a sentence   stamped out
the broadcast antenna broken   a sentence

3.

written over our bodies   each of us
owns a few letters   this unread sentence   tense

        }

without the bodies proximate   we refuse   fuse
        & in the department for encouragement

        }

of children's art   the soldiers soiled the walls   all
with gouache & all the children's paintings

        }

smeared with urine & shit   they did their business
on the floors in the flowerpots in drawers in handbags

        }

in water bottles they did their business in photocopiers   ears
in sayings scrawled on walls   refuse & return   turn

        }

to sender   someone had forgotten his dog tags
you can read his name in the papers

        }

but not his whole name   & the sentence remains
unread   the address illegible   return to sender

Two States (Graduation Day, 2005)

In my haste, I sped   the Mach-3 Turbo
in the space between   my eyebrows

—which, over the   years, have grown,
inexorably, closer   together—unknown—

and nicked the skin,   and gouged out
a Gaza-sized beachhead   from one brow.

The arrogance of culture: to cultivate,
to uproot the follicles'

     wild delight,
to split apart by force   what leans together,
like glass
     and its shatter, like flesh
     and its suture.

In the photo, I stand   regalia-black and hooded
between two students on the DMZ between child- and adulthood

and between my eyes, an equal sign, a line
for each blade, (one blade
     missing),   the blood filling in behind.

Installation / Occupation

after Vera Tamari

1.

there was a time you couldn't paint   red white
green or black   could be a flag   imagine

you couldn't paint poppies or watermelon
now you can paint all you want   & yet this state

of uncertainty   will the doors hold out
can you leave your house can you walk around

this occupation   when the tanks come
crack down   drive the sidewalks for fun   for weeks

all these smashed cars lining the city streets
my friend's red Beetle   flipped over   its legs in the air

so in a field   we paved a road to nowhere   & placed
the crushed   in a column   as if in a rush hour

line of traffic   we had an opening   at our piece
a huge party on our road   & then walked home

2.

before dawn a column of Merkavas
came back   my house was opposite the field

& I could see the tanks pull up   & yield
two heads emerged from turrets   trying to read

the scene   then went back inside the hatch
& ran over the exhibit   over & over

again backwards and forwards   then shelled it
& for good measure christened it with piss

I caught it all on video   this metamorphosis
of the piece   there's the story of Duchamp

once the workmen installing his exhibit
dropped a crate of paintings   the floor

shattering the glass   Duchamp ran over
thrilled   now he said   now it is complete

The Ash Tree

December, 1998

1. *On I-90 in Indiana, Driving Westward*

Just before we shoot through Gary,
>   our '84 Accord stutters, lurches
>   and goes silent. Only the radio chatters,

like someone beginning to freeze,
>   of the latest surgical strike: Operation
>   Desert Fox. Last night, we held hand-

scrawled signs at Courthouse Square, lifting
>   gloved slogans against the awestruck
>   exclamations of CNN. The gaggle

of traffic responded: quick beeps, long honks,
>   the bird. One Ram Tough guy bleated
>   something about Iraq, the Stone Age.

Like a small rain falling,
>   Hassan said of the bombing. Flurries
>   blow like flies into headlights,

all America catapults into winter.
>   On the radio an Ojibway singer
>   says the drum is the heart

of the people. When the drum stops,
>   the people die. In the breakdown lane
>   outside the Murder Capital of the World,

we consider the risks: stay in the car—
        frostbite or mangled metal. Flag down
                some help—robbery at gunpoint. Descend

the exit ramp curling beneath us,
        to call a tow— . . . .
                . . . . Headlights

bulldoze the black ash of Indiana night.

2. *Winter Solstice, Lincolnshire, Illinois*

Dawn. In this suburban preserve,
        I skid down the icy driveway in skivvies
for the news, swaddled in blue plastic.
        No mention of the midnight angel

descending in greasy overalls to lay
        his gnarled hands on our dead engine.
Overhead, Canada geese kvetch
        like families parting at an airport gate.

Tomorrow, when you fly home,
        you'll still be with me
like my own pulse, beating
        its single wing in my wrist:

what the geese ululate over,
        what the robed Iraqi wonders

in the *Tribune* photo: he clasps
       his daughter's hand, stares down a crater

where his house had been. My love,
       this is our country. A small rain falls,
arrowheads of birds arc the sky. Last spring,
       they circled our familiar ash tree

my father had just hacked to kindling.
       It took him all day, what had been dying
from within for years. What stood
       cock-eyed and etched on my childhood

window, now hisses in our hearth, rages
       beyond all protest: the ash tree
squat in the flames it feeds
       with itself, burning into its name.

III

The best way to treat a death . . .
swallow the illustrious dead.

VINCENT VAN GOGH
(Arles, Feb. 1888) to Theo

St. Basil

And he said, "go and say to the people:
Hear, but do not understand.
See, but do not perceive."

ISAIAH 6:9–10

Forget the postcard St. Basil's, its cupolas
swirled ice cream sold on Red Square. Forget
the postcard, cupolas like fireworks
frozen in burst, colored onions pulled
up by unseen hands. Past the Tsar's bell—
too huge to use, only echoing now
the tour guide's canned prattle

to Pushkin Square's McDonald's.
The gypsy children sing their parts in a play
for pity. Rouged with dirt, they dance,
thrust a newborn at a tourist—her hands full,
they empty her pockets and run. Nearby,
a blind drunk's trembling palms
part the crowd, knock on car windows

like stunned birds. The city's too much.
I take an outbound, wedge between
a babushka's bloated coat, a mafia tough's
sleek leather. Cut a circle from steamy glass:
dim outlines of trees, unfinished apartments
decay, windows boarded. On unlit platforms,
people feel their way, their arms extend

against station buildings, feathered
by paper-scrap ads. In the bitter wind, walls
flutter and whip: *Exchange apartment?*
Call Dmitry. Notice. Have Moskvich, will sell.
Tracks end. A rusted kiosk, empty as a socket
where an eye had been. The sky stretches
past all imagining. What did I come here for?

Bear-thick workers sprawl in sleep,
orange overalls smeared with soot.
Cabbages in sacks hang on coat hooks,
sleeping heads loll to the rocking.
In the opposite seat, a child's dusty palms
in a fist, as if to hide something hard.
His father's face a posthumous book.

He looks at me. Outside, light knifes between
trees. At this speed, they flatten, bend
around the corners of vision. A single tree
enlarges. Freezes. Distends, until I turn
away. Like the hunched backs
of babushkas, bodies carrying years
like oaks, every winter thickening limbs.

I wake: Moscow. And return again,
in dreams, to what I could not complete,
could not forget: the man I tripped over—
frozen, half-naked, his bloody mouth still
wincing red. And those who opened
their doors like family secrets in Monino,
Oktyabrskoye Polye, Taganka—stairs

to a floor never built. In winding streets
of dreams, I can almost hear Napoleon's gasp
at a people willing to burn the city to keep it
from him, the Tsarina's secret purr
at Potemkin's prop-towns built to impress
foreign guests. On the Volga, a church shimmers
its liquid reflection, glossy

as photos I glance through, looking
for Moscow. Already it slips from me,
the bundled crowd crossing the square,
sweet cigarettes, car fumes and sweat jostling
the bells tolling through Siberian air,
the name of the idiot healer I needed,
never found. He'd dip a coal in water,

touch the face. His mangled mouth offered
no words. Walked naked in snow, impervious
to those who beat him, until people believed him
holy. When he died, Ivan the Terrible
wept bitterly: the seizured frothing mouth
now bronzed into icon. St. Basil,
Basil the fool, bloomed into cupolas.

On 24th and South, Philadelphia

We need to envision utopia,
I read today, just before we heard
the crash outside.

We need to envision utopia
but tonight, love, we gape
at the wind-blasted craters and cliffs
of Arctic ice
filmed in *Nanook of the North*. Nanook, nearly
on all fours, gnaws
the frozen leather of his boots—
just to walk outside. His wife cuts an igloo window

out of ice. Today, we saw a woman's face
sculpted into windshield.
She stumbled from the car, holding her head
like a bell. Someone brought her a blanket,
lay her down. Broken,
the traffic light closed its eye. We stood,
the whole street still
crowded, quiet, someone sweeping glass,
red lights pulsing over everything.
I can't help but admire
Smailović, dressed in full concert attire,

carefully stepping to the bottom
of a Sarajevo bomb crater, pulling the bow
across his cello
twenty-two days, one day for each one dead—
too often, I long for another's life.

But sometimes, you call me out
of myself so completely, I cease
turning from what's right
in front of me. Some kids craned out a third story window,
Bomb Pops dripping to the street. Together
we watched the woman's boyfriend
pound on the ambulance door
where the world lay, shaken, amnesiac, wanting him.

Hiroshima: A Panorama

September 1945

The old scrolls were opened
        but never all at once,
so the eye would wander
        over the course of months

each inked and painted shrub,
        each circuitous path,
and never know where
        it might lead—so hang back,

rest awhile in thickets
        of this imagined world,
a landscape where only
        a hand-span unfurled

at once, and soon, the left half
        would disappear, a new
half, always facing east
        would swim into view.

Here, the panorama lies
        whole, defeated, splayed
wingless on the wall—
        the modest houses

mere footprints, suggestions
        of foundations, trees
stripped to the dead trunk,
        and you hardly notice

the slight shadows leaning
        down the main road,
as if drawn to something
        that cannot be found

by the naked eye, scanning
        from such distant height
the landscape all at once—
        a single instant of light.

The Idle Childless

The largely-unpuked-upon
dine in Thai Gardens every Friday night,
decide between Mango Lassi or Mai Tai,
discuss the tonal color of their favorite
Tuvan throat singers, Huun-Huur-Tu,
and lose a whole hour plotting
their annual worldspinning travel—

whose thoughts saunter like couples
on the observation deck of a cruise,
stand chatting before the banquet table,
freshened drinks in hand,
who can retire to bed whenever they choose,
with whomever they choose,
and wake whenever they can no longer

sleep—who, upon waking, occasionally
wonder what it was they'd forgotten,
the thread of it left behind in a dream,
and though they tug at it, it unhooks itself,
slips off, like a pair of glasses
over the ship's railing, and sinks
to the bottom of whatever ocean they float over.

Negatives

Jogging to pick up the X-rays of my mouth,
I squint against the lancing sun, houses
jutting along the road.

And then I see the yellow cordon,
two cops talking to neighbors. A small group
gathers, gaping, silent.

One cop swaggers into the alleyway,
the walkie-talkie rasping in his belt
like a gramophone,

and drapes the sheet over the crushed body.
The cop points three floors up. She signed her name
in air, disappeared.

I get the X-rays—no toothaches yet,
just the slow shading of decay, a ghost
of molar capped with gold,

roots, gums wearing away. I fast-forward
through the paper for a name, a story
to wedge between the body

and my eye. I find none.
A crowd gathers around the cordon,
like a finish tape

the winner breaks. A rotting smell drifts
from steam grates. It's late, and the sun stabs
into X-rays. It's midnight,

rewind, play, rewind. Why did she dive?
The heart's iambics drill *not you, not you*
—until they wear a hole right through.

Creation Story on Magnolia Drive, Cleveland

The dregs of dried jasmine in the sink, pear slices over flakes in a wooden bowl.

Once there was a woman floating in a cloud, looking down. Someone carrying a cello along the sidewalk, against the wind, as if she were dragging a partner in a marathon

dance, trying not to fall. Once a car turned over, woke from its dream, and wandered backward down the drive. Once a turtle sat sunning in the middle of the street, neck outstretched, eyes closed, holding up the world.

Once there was a nickel, a dime, slipped into the parking meter: fifteen minutes of borrowed time. Fennel spines sticking out of a paper sack, a drought-split tomato bigger than a fist. Our local gangster, gold chains around his neck, cradled the cardboard carton, fingered each egg for cracks.

Mid-morning drizzle, back home, you talking pathology blues to your sister on the phone. And wind shushing the willows. On the floor below, the Greens outlining the risks of transporting plutonium. And wind shushing the willows. Dumping the rancid vegetables in the backyard. A stopped-up toilet, rising out of itself.

And wind shushing through willows, working to strip the branches bare. Upon a time once. Once there was she, once there was me, and not yet three: oil of safflower, sweet almond and sesame. (*I was falling.*) And lovely flanks, and a rough tongue tracing a flower. (*She was falling.*) Calendula and rosemary: not yet three. (*You were falling, falling.*) And downstairs, someone cleaning dishes in a kitchen.

And hair sweeping over legs like a silk fan. And thunder, and thunder, lightning falling, and a ripple and shudder of the blinds, O and O and O—wind breathing sweet magnolia.

Nicodemus Below the Cross: A Votive Ivory

Because the dead grow so heavy, as if
        wanting the earth
below them, and because we cannot stand
        the sight of them,

their gravity, we leave the gravesite even
        before the hole
is filled with dirt. You refuse to leave
        your dead father.

From the silence of our car, we look at you,
        sobbing. No sounds
reach us. Your face wild with rage. You hold
        your own body,

leaden, armed, your fingers rub beneath your eyes,
        as if to wear away
what lay before us. In the votive,
        it's so easy

to mistake Nicodemus for the crucifier,
        his hammer poised
over Christ's ivory wrists, his face blurred
        with fear. His hand

will strike the nail away, hold the body until
        blood runs its course,
then lay it down. In the votive, the last flecks
        of olive, dun, and red

—the artist's paints—river the veins
        of the deepest cuts
only. No thorns of gold, no gem-encrusted
        cross, no tesserae-

shattered image of a god. Just a body
        cradling a body
carved in elephant's tusk, small enough
        to carry. An ancestry

of hands worrying, worrying the ivory
        features smooth.

Antibodies (for Adele)

First Day.

And there was bilirubin.
Protean creature, already

the first war of your blood,
antibodies and dying cells.

Let there be light then, isolette
and velcro restraints—

intensive but mother-close,
milk and honey of the body.

Already you labor
to throw off the yoke,

the blindfold strapped to protect
your alien eyes

from a light that just might
disarm your blood.

Second.

Rolling squalls
subsided, you recede

into the shell of yourself,
away from the rat's nest

of wires taped and suctioned
to a fetal body not yet

yours, never ours. Already
the thick thirst to pray:

to say *come back*
to your body, so curled

into itself, as if you've
moved to higher ground.

Unsuture those closed lids.
Bring back your storms.

Third.

Heat-greedy, sun-bather,
we take you home

in a glowing blanket
trailing a hose tail

plugged into a box that hums
like a slide projector—

space child so soon
from the cord, you've grown

another. Dark-starved,
drunk insomniacs,

our days turned inside-
out, we wide-eyed

crowd around, luxuriate
in your ultraviolet night.

Fourth.

They prick your heel
each day, suck the blood

like poison from a snakebite.
The snake's already inside.

They will read the blood
drawn from you, each daily poke

probing the undiscovered
wormholes of our body,

hidden like a language
we didn't know we understood.

The nurse regrets your silence
on the matter—*The blood*

comes faster when you cry,
she says, readying the gouge.

Fifth.

In an elevator descending
I find myself rocking to sleep

a Tupperware of roasted potatoes
on a bed of rosemary

cradled to my chest.
My little potato, you've taught

me never to stop moving.
You swim in my arms,

sea anenome, perpetual motion
machine of the limbs,

your muscles twitching on
marionette strings of your own

desire, surf through the breakers
of pure air.

Sixth.

Eden was the bed
we daily made

away from the dirt and ache
of work, labored to make

the salty sap of the day
sweet between us. Today,

the gate of fatigue grows
like a sudden tree, and we know

it's too late—too early?—
and this daughter, this lovely

one slithers in honey-stung
skin, applies herself to the apple

of the breast, her tongue
coaxing your nipple.

one more story he said In a restaurant
in Amsterdam

a young woman came in
speaking Arabic I said are you Iraqi
she said I haven't eaten for three days
I said what do you mean she said
I need to turn turn myself in
this was a strange language to me
a different logic Come and sit I said
food brought out she ate finally
spoke her husband now in Istanbul
they'd escaped Iraq he was taxi driver
sold his car paid $5,000 to Turkish driver
to send her Istanbul to Amsterdam
a big truck crates of fruit and vegetables
had a tiny space   in the middle kept her
there gave her food and water supposed to last
seven days lasted four strange language
mouth of the truck she was stuck
in one position for seven days could not
move crates of figs pallets cracked
blocked lodged then they just dropped her
in the middle of Amsterdam right then she was
hoping waiting turn myself in my husband not
far behind strange language to me I did not
understand turn myself in in the middle
of Amsterdam do you speak speak

For the Fifty (Who Made PEACE with Their Bodies)

1.

In the green beginning,
      in the morning mist,
            they emerge from their chrysalis

of clothes: peel off purses & cells,
      slacks & Gap sweats, turtle-
            necks & tanks, Tommy's & Salvation

Army, platforms & clogs,
      abandoning bras & lingerie, labels
            & names, courtesies & shames,

the emperor's rhetoric of defense,
      laying it down, their child-
            stretched or still-taut flesh

giddy in sudden proximity,
      onto the cold earth: bodies fetal or supine,
            as if come-hithering

or dead, wriggle on the grass to form
      the shape of a word yet to come, almost
            embarrassing to name: a word

thicker, heavier than the rolled rags
      of their bodies seen from a cockpit:
            they touch to make

the word they want to become:
        it's difficult to get the news
                from our bodies, yet people die each day

for lack of what is found there:
        here: the fifty hold, & still
                to become a testament, a will,

embody something outside
        themselves & themselves: the body,
                the dreaming disarmed body.

2.

And if the exposed
        flesh of women spells,
                as they stretch prone, a word

they wish the world
        might wear, the tenderness
                of unbruised skin, juice

of itself unsipped? And then?
        Here, where flesh is marked
                & measured in market

scales of the ogler's eyes,
        will they fall, cast down
                to their own odd armor,

or gloat on the novel glut
        of flesh, the body commodity
                no Godiva can set free?

But what if unbuffed generals,
        grandfathers unashamed, stood
                before camera's judgment,

vulnerables genuflecting
        to the cold, their sag noses
                shying from all eyes—

unjockstrapped, uncupped,
        an offering of useless nipples
                & old maps of animal fur

tracing their chests? It's no use.
        Shoot out the lights, suture
                the lids, & trace with fingertips

the blind-dark rooms
        of what we are, houses
                of breath, sheltered & unshelled.

Bat Suite

First the black swoop
        around our ears, then panic

fluttering in our chests.
Then nothing. A house

        with an uninvited guest,
not bothering to knock,

who plunks himself down
        wherever he wants, and he wants

somewhere upstairs.
There. Like a dirty wet rag

        drying, it hangs black, inverted, its claws
gripping a window screen darkened

by the shade of firs.
        I nudge its pink nose

with a tennis racquet. It bares
its fangs in a hiss

        my ears can't hear.
It would be so easy to crush. I'm told

the last man for the job
        whacked it like a ball

that happened to have wings.
It takes off—pulsing—beating—the air

      sliding feinting   darting
like sudden weather. Like

last night, my infant daughter trying
      to shed her skin with each yowl,

some unknown pain
whirling before her

      like blind night, blinder
and wider than the huge eye

of the lake we drove around,
      numbed to her cries,

helpless to end them.
There is no poetry in this:

      how once, addled by lack
of sleep, my wife carrying our daughter down-

stairs, tripped on a vacuum's
      umbilicus, and tumbled,

Adele falling   out of our arms—
the sickening crack

                   of her head on the landing.
The no sound.

Then the keening sound, carrying
                   over the mirror of the lake.

So easy to crush. Wielding a vintage
wooden tennis racquet

                   and window screen as a shield,
I tilt and stumble as the bat

whirls its unpredictable
                   orbit. Our daughter's cries

will turn to sleep, cradled
between us in our bed. The bat

                   will glide, suddenly,
through the yawning window

it had flown past a dozen times
                   before. But right now,

my in-laws gathered on the floor
below, listen on the baby monitor

                   as if to some broadcast
of a serial thriller—The Lone Ranger

or The Fat Man, or some update
        on the War—as I crash

and chuckle and keep my eyes
locked onto a fluttering

        hand that offers itself
neither in aid nor in greeting,

just itself, turning on invisible
        marionette strings

of sound, conductor and orchestra
for a suite

        above our human octaves.

NOTES

3   **Primer for Non-Native Speakers**   Derived in part from
Russian conversation primers, called *razgovorniks*, and Russian
language textbooks.

In Russian, there are simple comparative and compound com-
parative adjectival forms. This poem collapses that grammatical
form with the experience of comparing nations: "with you (your
country), everything is good, but with us, everything gets worse
and worse."

"They beat you because of your face, not because of your pass-
port" refers to a Russian saying.

Apparently, Yuri Gagarin's spaceship (which orbited the earth in
1961) was not seen by the public during the Cold War.

11   **Ashberries: Letters**   For Amy Breau.

The typical Russian phrase used to denote "outside," when
one speaks of weather, for example, is . . . "on the street," or
"in the yard."

Alyosha (Lyosh)—my "little brother" in the Maslov family, with
whom I lived for a few months in 1992, during the early post-
Soviet period, when the economy was in near-total collapse.

A *dvornik* is a yardkeeper. During the Soviet period, many
writers were forced into manual labor jobs to punish them
for writing; later, writers often chose those jobs to opt out
of the system.

14 **Ashberries: A Spectroscopy** A version of this poem was published as the note to the poem in *Best American Poetry* (2002).

Art historians and conservators have employed spectroscopic X-ray techniques to expose the layers of paint beneath a work of art.

The town where I lived was Kaliningrad, a suburb of Moscow. I learned recently that its name has been changed to Korolev. That Kaliningrad no longer exists.

15 **Days of 1993** is for Capt. Philip Metres, Jr., my father, who served in the Vietnam War as a Naval Advisor and lived through the Tet Offensive.

During the early post-Soviet years in Moscow, there were almost no public places where one could sit down inside during the winter months. The McDonalds on Pushkin Square, ironically, was one of the few downtown locations were I could get out of the cold.

18 **Yuri Gagarin's Spaceship** Yuri Gagarin was the first man in space, and the first to orbit the earth. He died in a plane crash in 1968.

In Russian, the words *Sputnik, Vostok, Soyuz,* and *Mir* mean traveler, east, union, and world or peace, respectively.

Baba Yaga is a witch from Russian folklore who lives in a hut that moves on chicken's legs; this hut is known to hold a palace inside.

20 **Matryoshka, Memory** is for Henry Frederick Dannemann, Jr., my grandfather, and my brother, David Metres.

In Russian, the words for "rain" (*dozhd'*) and "waiting" (*dozhdat'*) echo, as do "umbrella" (*zont*) and "horizon" (*gorizont*).

24 **Echolocation Islands** is for John Patton.

There is no place called Echolocation Islands. The epigraph was found in the "Echolocation" article on wikipedia.org.

Losiny Ostrov, or Elk Island, the first national park designated in Russia, is located in the northern suburbs of Moscow. It is not surrounded by water; in the old days, the woods located between fields and towns were called islands. Large part of this forest were destroyed during the Second World War, when the Soviet Army maneuvered its tanks around Moscow through the woods. These places were replanted after the war.

Solovki is an island in the White Sea, located near Arkhangelsk where, during the Soviet period, a notorious concentration camp existed on the grounds of a Russian Orthodox monastery.

27 **From Sokolniki** is for Jeremy Huck.

I could not track down the name of the author of the one-word book.

28 **Reunion: Insomnia Dacha** is for Dmitry Psurtsev, the Psurtsev family, and the "den of the voice."

"*around the table/we share/pure spirits*" is my translation of a haiku by Estonian poet Arvo Mets.

The poem plays on rhymes and roots in Russian words. In Russian, "monument" (*pamyatnik*), for example, contains "memory" (*pamyat'*). The word *soznaniye* can mean both "consciousness" and "conscience," and *bezsonnitsa* can mean both "sleepless" and "dreamless."

40 **Letter to My Sister** is for Katherine Metres Abbadi and Majed Abbadi.

Thanks to "Manal" and "Ashraf" for their testimony.

43   **Making Meshi** is for Philip and Lily Metres, who sleep in death.

Lily spent her childhood in Haiti, and a French convent in Beirut, before moving to Brooklyn. Philip spent his childhood in Mexico.

Meshi, or *mahshi*, is the Arabic word for "stuffed," here refers to stuffed grape leaves, what is commonly referred to as "dolmas."

Hudda means "shit."

45   **The Ballad of Skandar** is for my ancestor, Skandar ibn Mitri Abourjaili.

47   **A House Without** is for Lily Boulos and the family (especially Philip, Richard, John, Lila, and Salma) at 290 Hicks Street.

51   **The Familiar Pictures of Dis**   Many of the details come from a news story by Israeli journalist Amira Hass.

55   **Installation/Occupation**   Much of the language here is from Vera Tamari, an artist in Ramallah.

During the early years of the Israeli occupation of the West Bank and Gaza Strip, strict controls were placed upon artists and writers; even the word *Palestine*—not just the colors of the flag (red, white, green and black)—was forbidden.

The Merkava is a battle tank of the Israeli Defense Forces.

57   **The Ash Tree** is for Amy Breau.

Operation Desert Fox was the name of the U.S. campaign in Iraq in December 1998.

The Murder Capital of the World refers to Gary, Indiana.

63   **St. Basil** is for the Maslovs and Olga Leontevna.

Based in part on the story of Basil the Blessed, one of the *yurodivy* ("holy fools") who were held in esteem in old Russia.

67 **On 24th and South, Philadelphia**   While reading Fredric
Jameson's *Postmodernism: The Cultural Logic of Late Capitalism*,
where, later, we would read his desire "to enable a situational
representation on the part of the individual subject to that
vaster and properly unrepresentable totality."

Vedran Smailović was the Sarajevan cellist who played his cello
for 22 days to honor the 22 people who had been killed by
Serbian forces while queuing for bread.

69 **Hiroshima: A Panorama**   Based on a panoramic photograph
of Hiroshima taken weeks after the atomic bomb was dropped,
as well as Japanese scrolls on exhibit at the Cleveland Museum
of Art.

74 **Creation Story**   Thanks to the Cleveland Friends Meeting.

76 **Nicodemus Below the Cross: A Votive Ivory** is for my mother,
Kay Metres.

Based on a votive ivory from the Byzantine period. The
Nicodemus figure that appears in the votive is apparently
apocryphal.

78 **Antibodies (for Adele)** is for my daughter, Adele Frances Breau
Metres.

83 **one more story he said In a restaurant in Amsterdam**
Thanks to Kadhim Shabaan for his witness during the late
1990s in Iraq.

84 **For the Fifty (Who Made PEACE with Their Bodies)** is for
the Baring Witness movement, begun in 2002, to demonstrate
against the Bush Adminstration's War On Terror. This poem
also appeared as a broadside by Twin Cranes Press in 2004.

87 **Bat Suite** is for my in-laws, Ted and Fran Breau.

Recent Cleveland State University Poetry Center Titles

Nin Andrews. *The Book of Orgasms*

Dan Bellm. *Buried Treasure*

Christopher Burawa. *The Small Mystery of Lapses*

Jared Carter. *Les Barricades Mystérieuses*

John Donoghue. *A Small Asymmetry*

Patrick Michael Finn. *A Martyr for Suzy Kosasovich*

Diane Gilliam Fisher. *One of Everything*

Max Garland. *Hunger Wide as Heaven*

Douglas Goetsch. *The Job of Being Everybody*

Gaspar Pedro Gonzalez. The Dry Season

Susan Grimm, ed. *Ordering the Storm: How to Put Together a Book of Poems*

Linda Lee Harper. *Kiss, Kiss*

Jayson Iwen. *A Momentary Jokebook*

Sarah Kennedy. *Double Exposure*

Karen Kovacik. *Metropolis Burning*

George Looney. *Attendant Ghosts*

Alison Luterman. *The Largest Possible Life*

Helena Mesa. *Horse Dance Underwater*

Henri Michaux. *Someone Wants to Steal My Name*

Bern Mulvey. *The Fat Sheep Everyone Wants*

Deirdre O'Connor. *Before the Blue Hour*

Carol Potter. *Short History of Pets*

Barbara Presnell. *Piece Work*

Mary Quade. *Guide to Native Beasts*
Tim Seibles. *Buffalo Head Solos*
Tim Seibles. *Hammerlock*
Ruthanne Wiley and Eric Anderson. *Duo: Novellas*
Eliot Khalil Wilson. *The Saint of Letting Small Fish Go*
Sam Witt. *Sunflower Brother*
Margaret Young. *Willow from the Willow*